HUMBLE PIE

HUMBLE PIE

GORDON RAMSAY

HarperCollins*Publishers*

HarperCollins*Publishers*
77–85 Fulham Palace Road,
Hammersmith, London W6 8JB

www.harpercollins.co.uk

Published 2008

1

A CIP catalogue record of this book
is available from the British Library

ISBN-10 0-00-727096-8
ISBN-13 978-0-00-727096-5

Printed and bound in Great Britain by
Clays Ltd, St. Ives plc

Mixed Sources
Product group from well-managed
forests and other controlled sources
www.fsc.org   Cert no. SW-COC-1806
© 1996 Forest Stewardship Council
FSC

To Mum, from cottage pie to *Humble Pie*
– you deserve a medal.

Contents

Foreword

In my hand, I've got a piece of paper. It's Mum's handwriting, and it's a very long list of all the places we lived until I left home. It's funny how few of them I can remember. In some cases, that's because we were hardly there for more than five minutes. But in others, it's because, as a boy, I was often afraid and ashamed, and always poor. And you don't dwell on the details of a house if you connect it with being afraid, or ashamed, or poor.

I don't think people grasp the real me when they see me on television. I've got the wonderful family, the big house, the flash car. I run several of the world's best restaurants. I'm running round, cursing and swearing, telling people what to do. They probably think: that flash bastard. But my life, like most people's, is about hard work. It's about success. Beyond that, though, something else is at play. I'm as driven as any man you'll ever meet. When I think about myself, I still see a little boy who is desperate to escape, and keen to please. I just keep going, moving as far away as possible from where I began. Work is who I am, who I want to be. I sometimes think that if I were to stop working, I'd stop existing.

This, then, is the story of that journey – so far. I'm just forty-one, and it seems, even to me, such an amazing and long journey in such a short time.

Will I ever get there? You tell me.

Chapter One

Dad

The first thing I can remember? The Barras in Glasgow. It's a market – the roughest, most weird place, full of second-hand shit. In a sense, I had a Barras kind of a childhood.

Until I was six months old, we lived in Bridge of Weir, a comfortable, leafy place just outside Glasgow. Dad, who'd swum for Scotland at the age of fifteen, was a swimming baths manager there. After that, we moved to his home town, Port Glasgow, where he was to manage another pool. Everything would have been fine had he been able to keep his mouth shut, but Dad was a hard-drinking womanizer and competitive, as much with his children as with anyone else. And he was gobby, very gobby.

Mum is softer, more innocent, though tough underneath. She's had to be. I was named after my father, but I look more like her – the fair hair, the squashy face. I have her strength, too – the ability to keep going, no matter what life throws at me.

Mum can't remember her mother at all – my grandmother died when she was just twenty-six, and Mum wound up in a children's home.

At sixteen, she began training as a nurse. One Monday night, she got a pass so that she could go dancing with a girlfriend of hers. A man asked Mum to dance, and that was my father. He played in the band, and she thought he was a superstar.

When she turned seventeen, they married – on 31 January 1964 in Glasgow Registry Office. There were no guests, no white dress for her, and nothing doing afterwards, not even a drink. His father was a church elder. Kissing and cuddling were strictly forbidden. About two weeks after she was married, Mum's mother-in-law asked Mum if she was expecting a baby.

'No, I'm not,' said Mum, a bit put out.

'Then why did you go and get married?' asked her mother-in-law.

I've often asked Mum this question myself. I'm glad I'm here, of course, but my father was such a bastard that it's hard not to wonder why she stayed with him. Her answer is always the same.

'He wanted to get married, and I thought, "Oh, it would be nice to have my own home and my own children".'

Ten months later, my sister Diane came along and Dad got the job at a children's home in Bridge of Weir. According to Mum, it was lovely. Then it started – the drinking and the temper. He would slap her about.

Next was the job in Port Glasgow, but Dad was all over the place. 'Fed up,' he used to call it. And the womanizing got steadily worse. By now, Mum was pregnant with my brother, Ronnie. One morning, Dad came home and said that his car had been stolen. It was complete bollocks. What had actually happened was that he'd been with a woman, had a few drinks, and knocked down an old man in what amounted to a hit-and-run. We had to leave, literally, overnight.

My older sister, Diane, was toddling, I was in a pushchair, and Mum was pregnant. But did he care? No. It was straight on the train to Birmingham, and who knows why. It could just as easily have been Newcastle or Liverpool.

We found a room in a shared house. Amazingly, Dad only got probation and a fine for the hit-and-run, and he soon picked up a job as a welder and joined an Irish band. All the usual kinds of women were soon hanging on to his every word, and if he went out on a Friday night, you were lucky if you saw him again before Sunday.

Needless to say, the welding soon went by the way. He was convinced that he was going to be a rock and roll star. We'd go from market to market looking for music equipment, looking at these Fender Stratocaster guitars – the fucking dog's bollocks of the music world – and all our clothes were from jumble sales. How did he fund his shopping habit? He went to loan sharks, mostly. Because our names are the same, I'll sometimes get investigated by companies trying to get back the cash he owes them.

On birthdays, I used to get a £3.99 Airfix model kit from somewhere like the Ragmarket, Birmingham's version of the Barras. There'd be half of it missing, or the cardboard box it came in would be so wet and soggy that you wouldn't have wiped your arse with it.

Christmas was terrible. When we were older, Mum always used to work in a nursing home, doing as much double-time as she could. Sometimes she didn't even come home on Christmas Day. I used to dread Christmas. And then the bailiffs would show up. We'd be evicted. Dad's van would be loaded up, and we'd be off to the nearest refuge or round to the social services, pleading homelessness.

As a teenager, I used to be ashamed of some of the places we lived – the ones that were riddled with damp, the ones that had been left like pigsties by other families. And every time he got violent, any ornament, any present we'd bought for Mum, would be smashed, simply because it belonged to her.

For our schooling, we were never in one place long enough to develop any kind of attention span. Dad was hardly the kind of man to insist on you doing your homework. Only poofs did homework. The same way only poofs went into catering. No, he was much more interested in trying to turn us into a country music version of the Osmonds. Diane, Ronnie and Yvonne, my younger sister, all sing and play musical instruments. They didn't have any choice about that. Dad was obsessed. But I never went along with his plan. That's not to say I wasn't just as scared of him as they were. My tactic was to keep my head down and my nose clean. When I was asked to lug his bloody gear about the place, I just got on with the job. It's funny, really, that people think of me as so forceful and combative, because that's the precise opposite of how I was as a kid. I wouldn't have said boo to a goose.

His favourite punishment was the belt. You'd get whacked for something as innocent as drinking his Coke. I would get completely fucked over for that sort of thing. It wasn't so much the Coke he was bothered about, more that he wouldn't have a mixer for his precious Bacardi.

Yvonne was born in Birmingham. Next stop was Daventry, where we had quite a nice council house. Then we were off again, to Margate, where, for a time, we lived in a caravan. That was horrendous. We didn't even have enough money for the gas bottle to keep the place warm.

Then it was back up to Scotland again, followed by another stint in Birmingham, and then on to Stratford-upon-Avon. But Dad couldn't settle. Off he'd go: to France, or to America. He never sent money home. It was up to Mum to earn our keep. When he came back from abroad, we moved to Banbury, where he was going to run a newsagent's shop. We lived above the shop, and the guy who owned it was lovely. But Dad was on the fiddle. The owner found out, and we were out on our ears again.

So it was back up to Glasgow. But I was a teenager now, and I decided not to go. The council gave Diane and me a flat, and we stayed put. I was doing a catering course at college, funded by the local Round Table, but, in any case, I don't think Dad wanted either of us around.

I had crossed a line when I was fifteen. I was going out with a girl called Stephanie, and one night I came back late.

'Get your stuff out of my house, and go and live with her,' he said.

'I'm sixteen next week,' I said. 'I can go where I like.'

I'd already been given a big radio for the upcoming birthday, and he threw it at me from the top of the stairs.

'I can't believe you've done that,' I said. 'You know damn well that Mum bought it for me.'

I knew she'd got it on hire purchase, which was costing her £8 a month, and I couldn't bear it.

'I'd rather you did that to me than to something that hasn't even been paid for,' I said.

He came storming down the stairs. At first, I stood my ground. Then I saw the look in his eyes and I bolted. For the first time, I felt that he really might kill me. I saw something in his eyes that day – a kind of madness.

Once Diane and I were out of the way, he turned his madness to whomever else was there. Ronnie was his pal, mostly, so it was Yvonne's turn to take the treatment, and Mum was still getting knocked about. She was working in my

Uncle Ronnie's shop in Port Glasgow, and she'd come in with bruised lips and black eyes.

My uncle would say, 'Oh, Helen, you can't serve the customers looking like that!'

And she'd say, 'Well, it was your brother that did this to me.'

But no one intervened. Domestic violence was still seen as a private matter then.

Next, the four of them ended up in Bridgwater, in Somerset. It was there that he committed the final crime and left our lives – almost for good. It's a time I cannot think about without feeling the blood pulsing in my temples, though I wasn't even there when it happened.

Dad had had a couple of drinks, but this attack was planned – not some dumb, drunken rage. He came home from work, and Mum was in bed with a mug of hot milk. He poured it all over her, leaving bad scalding to her chest. Then he dragged her downstairs, and the beating started. By the time the ambulance arrived, her eyes were completely closed, her face swollen and pulped. First, she was taken to a hospital, then to a refuge. Dad, of course, disappeared at the first sound of a police siren.

That was when the social services and all the other authorities got fully involved, and a restraining order was taken out on him. He wasn't allowed anywhere near the house, but when Mum went home, she found everything that she had built up smashed into tiny pieces. He hadn't left even a light bulb intact. Worst of all, Dad had left a note on the mantelpiece. It read, 'One night, when you are least expecting it, I'll come back and finish you off.'

Dad went off to Spain, and I didn't see him for many years. Then, towards the end of 1997, when I was running a restaurant and already well-known, I got a call from Ronnie. Dad was in Margate. He'd had an argument with Anne, his second wife, and he'd upped and left. I called him on the number Ronnie had given me. I don't know why. He sounded very low.

'I'm here to see my doctor,' he said. 'Can I see you?'

'Yeah, yeah, I'll come down.'

It had been a difficult year. My wife, Tana, and I were expecting our first baby. And I was involved in all sorts of legal trouble over my restaurant. Still, I drove down there. There was something in me that couldn't refuse his request. I got out of my car and I saw this old, frail, white-haired man with bruises on his face, and marks on his knuckles. I felt stunned. This was the man I'd been scared of for so long, brought so low, so pathetic and feeble.

'What's happened to you?' I said.

'Oh, Anne and I separated, and I had an argument with one of her sons.'

'Look at the state of you. Where are you living?'

He pointed at the car park, and there was his Ford Transit van. Inside there were all his possessions and an inflatable camp bed in the back, with awful net curtains in the windows.

We had breakfast, and we went for a walk on the pier, and it was so sad. So I went to the bank and I got out £1,000, and I gave it to him for the deposit on a flat. I thought that at least I could do the right thing by him, and that's what he did. He got a little one-bedroom basement flat.

On Christmas Eve, he telephoned. Anne was coming over, and they were going to try and fix their problems. That was the last time I ever spoke to him.

After hearing that he and Anne had made up, I booked him a table at my restaurant for the twenty-first of January 1998. Most of my staff didn't even know I had a father. I'd reinvented myself, I suppose. I'm not ashamed of that. I've never tried to pretend anything else. All I knew was that I didn't want to be like him. And any time I came even close to that, I would put the fear of God into myself.

It was New Year's Eve when we heard that my father had died. I hated him, but still, his funeral was horrible. Anne organised it in a Margate crematorium that was so characterless, it might have been a branch of Tesco. We walked in, and his songs were playing. It was him singing. To me, that was the worst thing. And then there were so many strangers. We knew no one.

Mum didn't go, but my sisters and Ronnie did. By this time, Ronnie was a desperate heroin addict, and he had been refusing to go. I was at my wits' end. Finally, about an hour before the funeral, I gave him money so that he could buy what he needed to get him through it.

How low can you go? Very low indeed, if you're desperate.

I drove back to London and I went straight back to the kitchen, trying to think only about the next order. I don't think I've ever needed my kitchen so much in all my life.

What did my father leave me? A watch, actually. Everything else he 'owned' was on hire purchase. He never tasted my cooking.

'Cooking is for poofs,' he used to say. 'Only poofs cook.'

Chapter Two

Football

It was football, not cooking, that was my first real passion.

Football was one way I thought I could impress Dad. He and my Uncle Ronald were huge Glasgow Rangers fans, and I could see that this might be a way to reach him. I must have been about seven when I went to my first Rangers match. I remember being up on Ronald's shoulders and the amazing roar of the crowd. It was quite frightening.

Back in Stratford, I was chosen to play under-fourteen football when I was just eleven, and at twelve years old, I played for Warwickshire. Did I enjoy it? Yes, I loved it. And if Dad came to watch, it was a special relief, because at least that meant he wasn't at home giving Mum a hard time. He didn't always come to watch, though. Sometimes, he didn't even ask you the score. I got used to it.

Then, when I was fourteen, I went up to head a ball, and a miracle happened. The ball went straight into the back of the net. Unhappily along the way, the goalkeeper had managed to punch me in the stomach. I went down, and the referee came over, sat me up, and made me do all these sit-ups. I felt dizzy and weird. So he sent me off to get some water. I went to pee, and suddenly I was peeing blood, and two minutes later, I collapsed.

In the hospital, they thought it was my appendix. Then they thought it was a collapsed lung. That night, I was doubled-over in pain. I was in fucking agony. They took me down to surgery, and my spleen had been perforated. They managed to repair the damage, though they took my appendix out as well.

Two weeks later, an abscess developed internally. So it was back into hospital. This time, I had blood poisoning. All told, my recovery took three months from start to finish. I couldn't run, I couldn't jump and I couldn't train. And then, when I started kicking the ball again, I was nervous about going into a tackle. I had lost my confidence.

I remember my first serious game like it was yesterday. Dad was away, and you don't take your mum to football, do you? It was an English

Schools competition – Oxfordshire County against Inner London – held at Loftus Road, the ground of Queens Park Rangers, in London. It was amazing, and all the London players were from the youth teams of Chelsea, Tottenham and Arsenal. I thought we were going to get hammered, but we beat them 2–1. However, it was a dirty game. I was taken off after a bad tackle to my knee – another injury from which it took me ages to recover.

After I'd recovered, I played in an FA Cup youth game, and it was there that a Rangers scout spotted me. They asked if I'd like to spend a week of my next summer holiday with the club. Fucking hell! It wasn't just the fact that it was a professional club, it was RANGERS, the one club that would have an impact on the way Dad felt about me – or so I thought. By then, I was sixteen and was pushing the upper age limit for breaking into professional football. It was make-or-break time.

That first week was hard. I had an English accent, so they kicked the shit out of me for that. And they also made me use my right leg, which was fucking useless. We weren't allowed to rely on only one foot, in much the same way as, in the kitchen, you must be able to chop with both hands. Anyway, after that first week, I just hated Rangers.

I was called back three times. The process was horrible, and I was in two minds about begging for a fucking contract out of Rangers. I was settled in Banbury in the flat with Diane, and I was enjoying my freedom. I had my first serious girlfriend. I'd started working in a hotel. I had a bit of money, and there was always Banbury United if I wanted football. I got about £15 a game.

Mum phoned. She told me to contact my Uncle Ronald.

'Look, things have moved on,' he said. 'Rangers are going to invite you back up.'

He gave me a number to call. I phoned one of the head coaches.

He said, 'We want you back up. Can you bring your dad to training on May seventeenth?'

At that point, I wasn't even allowed to call the house. The trouble was that the people at the club wanted to know that I was properly supported.

I was thinking, 'Fuck, am I properly supported? No.'

I rang Mum and asked her to tell him. I couldn't face doing it myself.

So she did tell him, and, all of a sudden, he was ... not nice, exactly, but smarmy. He was going to enjoy my success as though he was me.

I played for the first team twice, in preseason friendlies, but it was a bad time for me. Dad's deceit was really getting to me.

Then they said, 'We're going to continue watching you. We're really excited. We are going to sign you – but it'll be next year, rather than this year.'

By this time, I'd been offered a cooking job in London. It was in a new 300-seater banqueting hall that had opened at the Mayfair Hotel. They were looking for four commis chefs: Second Commis, Grade Two. I don't know what the fuck that means, even now. It's a posh kitchen porter, basically, but the salary was £5,200 a year. Anyway, I told them that I could not start yet, and went back up to Rangers for the third year in a row.

This was the summer of 1984. Half the players weren't there because they were travelling in Canada, so everything was focused on the youth players. They were deciding who was staying and whom they were going to sign that year. Ally McCoist was there, and Derek and Ian Ferguson. They'd been involved with the club since they were boys, and I suppose that's all I ever really wanted to do, too: to stay put in one place, play football, and become a local boy.

The training went very well this time. I remember playing in a reserve team game against McCoist, and I had a good game. I was hopeful. I was feeling positive. The following week, we were playing a big charity match in East Kilbride. I couldn't believe it. I was in the squad, and I got to play. The trouble was that they kept moving me around the pitch. And then, to make things even worse, I got taken off fifteen minutes before the end. They must have made at least seven substitutions that day. Never mind. I trained for another two weeks, and then I played in another youth team match – another really good game. I was starting to think that I might be in with a chance.

Then came a disaster. In a training session, I seriously damaged my knee, and, stupidly, I tried to play on. We had to take penalties with our right feet. We each had to put a trainer on our left foot and a football boot on our right. The idea was to make your right foot work constantly. It must have been nearly four o'clock when they divided us into two teams and told us to play fifteen minutes each way and to give it 'everything you've fucking got'. By the time we finished, I was in serious pain.

I was out for eleven long weeks, but no sooner was I up and running again than I played a game of squash – a really dumb thing to do. I tore a ligament and was in plaster for four months. Once the plaster came off, I started training like a demon, but I was still in a lot of pain.

At the start of the season, there was no getting away from it. My leg was just not the same. Jock Wallace, the club's manager, and his assistant, Archie Knox, called me into their office one Friday morning. It was all over for me. I was not going to be signed. I remember their words coming at me like body blows. In those few minutes, all my dreams died. Part of me was wondering how I would manage to walk out of the room.

Telling Dad was one of the toughest things I have ever done, but I wouldn't let him have the pleasure of seeing me cry. On and on he went.

'You carry on badgering Rangers,' he said. 'You prove to them you are fit again.'

But far harder to take was his lack of sympathy for me. He didn't have a single kind word for me that day. Later on, he even suggested that I might be exaggerating the extent of my injury. So I went home, shut myself away, and had a good cry.

I suppose I mourned for what might have been. But I had to let go of the game that I loved. I was certain that I was doing the right thing in making a clean break. I had the example of my father and his so-called music career to encourage me, didn't I? There was no way I wanted to be a pathetic dreamer like him for the rest of my life. I wanted to be the best at whatever I did. The only question was: what would that be?

Chapter Three

Getting Started

When I was growing up, there wasn't a lot of money for food. But Mum was a good, simple cook: ham hock soup, bread and butter pudding, fish fingers, home-made chips and beans. We were poor, and the idea of having a starter, main course and pudding was unheard of. We were always on free school dinners, and on the last Friday of every month, the staff made a point of calling out your name to give you the next month's tickets. That was hell. It confirmed that you were one of the poorest kids in the class.

So I connected plenty of food with good times, with status. But I'd be lying if I said I was interested in cooking. I latched on to the idea of catering college because my options were limited, to say the least. I looked at the Navy and at the police, but I didn't have enough O levels to join either of them. So I ended up enrolling in a foundation year in catering at a local college, funded by the Rotarians. Did I dream of being a Michelin-starred chef? Did I fuck!

I remember coming home and showing Diane how to chop an onion really finely. I had my own wallet of knives. They had plastic banana yellow handles. At my restaurant in Chelsea, *Royal Hospital Road,* we wouldn't even use those to clean the shit off a pan. But I treated my knives and my white chef's clothes with love and reverence. I sent a picture of me in my big white chef's hat up to Mum in Glasgow. I was so fucking proud.

Meanwhile, I had a couple of weekend jobs. The first was in a curry house in Stratford, washing up. Then Diane got me a job working in the hotel where she was a waitress. Again, I was only washing up, but that was when I first got the idea of becoming a chef. I was in the kitchen, and I was in heaven.

After a year, one of my tutors suggested that I start working full-time, and attend college only on a day-release basis. I'd made good progress. So I started work as a commis at the place where I'd been washing up, the Roxburgh House Hotel. My first chef was this twenty-stone bald guy called Andy Rogers who would tell you off without ever explaining why. Dear God, you would not believe the kind of food that he got us to turn out. Roast potatoes started off in the deep fat fryer and were then sprinkled with Bisto granules before they went in the oven. This was to make sure they were nice and brown. We used to serve mushrooms stuffed with Camembert. I knew it was all dreadful, even then.

I was getting all this information at college, and I would come back and say, 'To make fish stock, you should only cook it for twenty minutes. Otherwise it will get cloudy. Then you should let it rest before you pass it through a sieve, or it will go cloudy again.'

For this, I would get roundly bollocked by the chef. He didn't give a fuck for college. I stayed for about six months, and then I got a job at a really good place called the Wickham Arms, in a small village in Oxfordshire. The owners were Paul and Jackie, and the idea was that I would live above the shop, which was a beautiful thatched cottage. Jackie was in her thirties. I must have been about nineteen. Paul was away a lot. Perhaps you can imagine what was going to happen.

One day, while Paul was off on one of his trips, Jackie rang down to the kitchen.

'Can I have something to eat?' she said.

'What would you like?'

'Just bring me a simple salad, thanks.'

So I got together a salad with a little poached salmon and took it up.

'Jackie, your dinner is ready.'

And she opened the door – stark bollock naked. I put the tray down, and went straight into her bedroom.

For the next six months, I led a kind of double life, and it was getting heavy. Jackie told me that she loved me. The truth is that I loved making the jugged hare more than I did having sex with the boss's wife, so I told them that I was leaving to go and work in London. She went bananas.

In the early part of 1998, they turned up at my restaurant, *Aubergine*. They'd opened a new restaurant, and they brought their chef to meet me. The trouble was, they got pissed and missed the train back to Buckinghamshire. We did try to ring around and find them a room, but hotels were £250 per night, which seemed to make them even angrier, so I sent out their dessert and then I fucked off.

At half past one in the morning, I got a call from Jean-Claude, my head waiter. He was screaming at me down the telephone. This chef of theirs was holding him over the bar, demanding that the arrogant fucker who left without saying goodbye – me – come on the line. About fifty minutes later, I rocked up on my motorbike and there was Mark, my head chef, fighting with Paul, and Paul's new chef fighting with Jean-Claude. They moved towards me before I had time to think.

Paul was going, 'I trusted you. How dare you? You shagged my wife!'

All my staff were thinking: WHAT? I could see it on their faces.

The resulting punch-up caused major head-lines when the Old Bill arrived. We all got taken off to make statements and then, when the whole thing was written up in the London *Evening Standard,* it was me who was supposed to have thrown all of the punches. It was all: 'I came to meet the great master and instead found an arrogant bastard,' 'Brawl that wasn't on the menu' and 'Ramsay punched my husband in the mouth.' I had to take legal action to clear that one up. I won, of course. As for Paul, he sent me a two-page fax apologising. That was the end of that.

To be fair, I don't really blame Paul for wanting to beat me up. Any man would have done the same in his position.

* * *

So I went to the starry lights of London. I was Second Commis, Grade Two, at the Mayfair Hotel, in its new banqueting rooms. I stayed about sixteen months, and I learned a lot. On my day off, I would work overtime without getting paid, just for the chance to work in the hotel's fine dining restaurant. It was a tough place. If someone called in sick, you could easily end up working a twenty-four-hour shift. You'd work all day in the restaurant, and then, during the night, you'd man the grill and do the room service. At half past four in the morning, all the Indian kitchen boys would sit down and have supper. Then they'd go and pray for an hour, and you'd already be preparing for the next morning's breakfast.

In those days, there was a really cool restaurant called *Maxine de Paris*, just off Leicester Square, and I'd heard that they were opening a new restaurant called *Braganza*. So I got a job there as a sort of third commis chef, but I didn't stay long. All the food went out by a lift between the kitchen and dining room, which meant it was always a bit cold, and I just couldn't come to terms with that. But there was an amazing chef there called Martin Dickinson, who'd worked at a restaurant called *Walton's*, a Michelin-starred place, and he was just great. I suppose that's when I realised that Michelin stars were the Holy Grail. The Michelin guides award one, two or three stars to the best restaurants around the world – three stars is the top award, and there are only three restaurants in the UK with three stars. As Martin had worked at a Michelin-starred restaurant, he seemed like a god to me.

'Get yourself into a decent kitchen,' he told me. 'Trust me, you don't want to be working in a place that serves smoked chicken and papaya salad. Get the fuck out of here.'

I went up to the staff canteen, which was just a grotty little room where all the chefs would smoke. I grabbed a magazine and I took it out into the garden in Soho Square.

'Christ,' I said to myself. 'There's Jesus.'

On the magazine's cover was a photograph of Marco Pierre White, all long hair and bruised-looking eyes. I was nineteen. He was twenty-five. He'd come from a council estate in Leeds.

When I looked at whom he'd worked with and where, I thought, 'Fuck me, he's worked for all the best chefs in Britain. I want to go and work with him.'

I phoned him up at his restaurant then and there.

'Where are you working now?' he said.

So I told him.

'Well, it must be a fucking shithole, because *Alastair Little* is the only place that I know in Soho. If you're not working there, then don't bother coming.'

So I told him that I was about to go to France because I wanted to learn how to cook properly.

'Have you got a job out there?' he asked.

'No, not yet.'

'Then come and see me tomorrow morning.'

I turned up at what would become the famous *Harvey's*, as requested. It had only been open about six months, and it would be another six months before it got its first Michelin star.

'Look,' he said. 'We work so fucking hard here. This kitchen will be your life. There's no social life, no girlfriends, and it's shit money. Do you want to leave now?'

'No, no. Not at all.'

So that was it. Next thing, he's telling me to get changed and come into the kitchen. He was making pasta. I'd never made pasta in my life. He showed me how to do a ravioli. He showed me how to do a tortellini. Then I had a go.

'Your fingers move fast,' he said. 'Do you want a job?'

'Yeah, I'd love a job.'

'You start Monday.'

'I've got to give a month's notice,' I said.

'Well, if you really want the job that fucking badly, you start Monday. What hours are you working?'

'I'm on earlies for the next month.'

Problem solved. I did the early shift at my old restaurant from 7 a.m. until 4 p.m. Then I got the tube to Victoria, and the train from there to Wandsworth Common, where I'd work at *Harvey's* until about two o'clock the following morning. It turned out that Marco's warning about the restaurant taking over my life was only the half of it.

* * *

In the beginning, I admired Marco more than I can say. His cooking left me speechless: the lightness, the control, the fact that everything was made to order. But it was the toughest place to work in that you could imagine. You had to push yourself to the limit every day and every night. A lot of the boys couldn't take the pace.

Marco was running a dictatorship: his word, and his word alone, was all that mattered. He had favourites, and then they would be out in the cold. He would abuse you mentally and physically. He would appear when you were least expecting him, silently, and his mood swings were unbelievable. One minute, he was all smiles. The next, he was throwing a pan across the kitchen. Often, the pan would be full. Stock went everywhere, or boiling water, or soup, but you wouldn't say anything. You'd wait for the quiet after the storm, and then you'd clear up, no questions asked.

The first time I saw Marco pummel a guy, I just stood there, my jaw swinging. I mean it. Jason Everett was physically beaten on the floor. We were all young and insecure, and Marco played on that. He'd find out about your home life while you stood there peeling your asparagus or your baby potatoes.

Then, four hours later, when you were in the middle of service and you'd screwed up, he would say, 'I fucking told you that you were a shit cook. You can't fucking roast a pigeon because you're too busy worrying about your mum and dad's divorce.'

Once, he was telling us all some crazy story about jumping off a train. Everyone was laughing, but then I said, 'Bullshit.'

He picked up his knife. Then he threw it down. Then he grabbed me and put me up against the wall. It was almost like being back at home with Dad. Maybe that's why I was able to put up with it for so long.

After Jason Everett had left, we were all in the shit. Working at *Harvey's* was physically tiring anyway, but once we were a man down, no one got any breaks at all. Then Marco called me upstairs to the office.

'I want you to do something for me,' he said. 'Jason is living in your flat, isn't he? Well, I've sacked him, and yet he's still in my kitchen. That's because, when you come into work in the morning, you've slept under the same roof. I want you to go home tonight and kick him out.'

I told Marco that I couldn't do this.

'Are you going to sack me?' I asked.

'Sit there,' he said.

The next thing I knew, he was on the phone. He rings some restaurant and says, 'Hi, John, it's Marco here. Look, I'm in the shit. My sous-chef [that was me] is being fucking awkward. So, John, three cooks next Monday.'

Then he put down the phone and said to me, 'You'll leave in a week's time. I want your notice.'

I went back downstairs.

'Everything okay?' said the guys.

'Yeah.'

I started making ravioli because, by then, I was completely running the kitchen. I finished the first one and then something in me just snapped. I hurled it at the wall. Fuck this, I thought. I walked out and I went to the train station, where I tore off my chef's whites and threw them in the nearest bin. I went back to the flat in Clapham.

'What are you doing here?' asked Jason. 'It's only six o'clock.'

'Get changed, mate. We're going to party. Marco's asked me to kick you out and I can't do that. He's told me I'm going in a week's time. Why should I wait a week?'

Fifteen minutes later, we're just getting changed when suddenly Steve Terry and another chef, Tim Hughes, and all the French waiters come in.

'Marco's closed the restaurant because you walked out,' said Steve.

I couldn't believe it. The restaurant manager had to ring all the customers to make excuses for Marco closing the restaurant.

It was a Saturday night. We NEVER had a Saturday night off. So we went to the Hammersmith Palais and we got totally pissed. The next night, we all piled off to a pub called The Sussex. All the chefs in London used to meet at The Sussex on a Sunday.

It was about nine o'clock when, all of a sudden, the music stopped and someone shouted, 'Is there a Gordon Ramsay in here?'

There was a phone call for me behind the bar. When I took it, a voice said, 'Gordon. Marco. I think we should talk.'

I told him that I was off to Tenerife the next day.

'What are you going to that shithole for?'

'Marco, after what you did to Jason and what you did to me, to be honest, I can't take it any more. You've pushed me to my limit.'

But he pushed some more, and I gave in. Why? The abuse I'd had from Dad had no point, but with Marco, the more tough he was on you, the more you felt yourself becoming better.

We arranged that I would meet him at *Harvey's* at midnight.

I walked into the restaurant. It was pitch black. When I switched on the lights, there he was, sitting in a corner of the room with a bottle of mineral water.

I started work again the next day.

How did he persuade me?

'Why are you throwing all this away?' he said. 'If you don't walk back into that kitchen tomorrow morning, you'll regret it for the rest of your life. I'll tell everyone that you ONCE worked here.'

Essentially, though, the climate of fear went on. He could be totally mad, but it was only when I worked in other seriously good kitchens that I realised that, despite his creative genius, Marco was unnaturally erratic.

Breaks were out of the question, mostly. The only way you could get one was to take your shallots and peel them while you were sitting out on the common. Woe betide you if he looked out and saw you kicking a ball around.

One day, he was going out for lunch with the chef and restaurant owner Albert Roux. That meant we had to do lunch on our own, something that really excited me. However, he said that he was going to make the sauces for that evening's dinner when he came back from lunch. I thought to myself: oh fuck, that means he's going to do the sauces just as we're going to slip out of the door for fifteen minutes. So I decided to do the sauces myself. I was so proud of them. About five minutes past twelve, he came to say goodbye. That's when he saw the sauces.

'What the fuck is going on here?' he said. 'Who finished those sauces?'

I put my hand up.

'Marco, it was me. I'm just about to bring them to the boil and cook them out for twenty minutes.'

Next thing you knew, pans were raining down on us. He went mad. I mean, fucking mad.

Finally, he threw the sauces themselves at us. That fucked up our fifteen-minute break, and it put us in the shit for sauces that night. I was gutted. There was nothing bloody wrong with those sauces. He didn't even taste them.

I stayed at *Harvey's* for two years and ten months. It was a massive learning curve for me, and it completely changed the way that I cooked. The trouble was that Marco made you feel as though there was nothing outside of *Harvey's* – that nowhere else mattered. That was just not true. Even if I hadn't been sick of the rages and the bullying, I needed to spread my wings if I was going to become the kind of cook I now so badly wanted to be. And that is exactly what I did next.

Chapter Four

French Leave

I landed a job with a top chef in Paris, but Marco wasn't having any of it.

'You're fucking stupid,' he said. 'Get yourself into a French kitchen in THIS country before you go off to France. I'll get you into *Le Gavroche*.'

Le Gavroche is a famous French restaurant in London. The man in the kitchen was Albert Roux. I didn't really want to work for Albert. Marco had worked for every top classical chef in the country including Albert, and now he could cook just as well as them. In turn, I'd taken everything I possibly could from him, so what would be the point of me going back to his teacher? On the other hand, it was exactly the kind of place I wanted to work in. And it was only open Monday to Friday. For the first time in my life, I'd be able to enjoy a proper weekend. Well, that was the theory.

I was in the shit, financially. When I got to Albert's restaurant, I said, 'I'm really pleased to be here. Thank you so much for allowing me to come here. Yes, sir, no, sir, three bags full, sir.'

Then I went straight back to being a commis chef. In other words, I was on less money and more in the shit than ever. So on Saturday nights, I would go back to *Harvey's* and work there so that Marco could take the night off.

It was very tough indeed. At Albert's restaurant, you had to be there at 6.30 a.m. You needed every bit of energy, and if you lagged behind, you were out on your ear. Michel, Albert's son, had worked out that I was working at *Harvey's*, too. He went mad, but he's an amazing guy. He lent me some money so that I didn't have to go to *Harvey's* any more.

'Look,' he said. 'Just pay me back later.'

At last, I could concentrate again.

Albert asked me if I would go and work with him at a place called Hotel Diva, a ski resort in the French Alps, in a place called Isola. I went for one season and it was amazing, a kind of working holiday. It was somewhere to start learning French, and to start understanding France. I was only twenty-three, and it seemed like a miracle. At Stratford High, lots of the kids would go off on skiing trips – but never us, because we couldn't afford it. Finally, I was skiing!

The kitchen was a challenge, as my French was so poor – I couldn't tell anyone what to do. Jean-Claude, who's now my head waiter at my restaurant *Royal Hospital Road,* worked at *Le Gavroche*. He came out to Diva with us, and he'd have to translate what customers said. But it was a great experience. There was a cookery school there as well, and people would ski during the day, take cookery lessons at night, and then enjoy a gourmet dinner.

One night, we had to put on an eight-course tasting menu for a massive group of *Mail on Sunday* readers. I was running the fish and the meat, and my head chef, Alan, was running the starter. It was a French fish stew. He'd made it that morning, but instead of putting it in the fridge to cool, he put it in these stainless steel buckets outside in the snow. The stuff was freezing over on the surface, while beneath, it was still warm. This made it fester.

Champagne and canapés were served, and everyone sat down for dinner.

'Fucking hell,' Alan said. 'Get me the starter, Ramsay.'

That was when he remembered that it was still outside. I scraped the ice off, pushed my fingers into a bucket, and it was horrible, like hot cheese. I came running in with the buckets.

'You'd better take a look,' I said.

Then in walks Albert, screaming that he wants to taste a cup of the stew.

Then, rather than admit his mistake, Alan brought it to the boil, skimmed off the froth and the natural yeast, and tipped in a bit of brandy. Then he gave it to Albert. Well, fuck me. He went ballistic. He got hold of the bucket and he just threw it. He was aiming for Alan, but it was the kitchen porter who took most of it. There was saffron and tomatoes bubbling across every wall.

What happened next? Albert went out and made a speech. And while he made that speech, we made fish stew from scratch. I spread it between six pans, and there were fourteen of us dashing between them, crushing it, blitzing it and skimming it – eighty portions in all. What a nightmare!

* * *

From the ski slopes, I made my way – at last – to Paris. There, I went down to an even lower salary, but believe me, as a Brit in a French kitchen, they weren't going to pay me proper money. It worked out at about £480 a month.

My first job was at the *Guy Savoy* restaurant, which had two Michelin stars. There, I learned total respect for food, and how you can make something out of nothing. Take a leek. At *Harvey's*, we would take a fourteen-inch leek and use half an inch of white stuff to finish a soup. The rest of it would be binned. In France, you'd use the best white bit for the soup, but then you'd use the rest for a sauce, and the very top in a staff meal. Nothing went in the bin. It was all about precision and freshness. My eyes were opened by the way that they roasted the most amazing capons and guinea fowl, and by the way the chef would order in such small quantities: sixteen tomatoes, or a dozen shallots, or just two sea bass.

* * *

It took me three months to get upstairs. They put me on fish, one of the most difficult stations of all. It was a baptism of fire. Fish demands precision. Thirty seconds' too much cooking can mean that bass is dry, ruined. But the minute I was there, I was away, there was no stopping me. I swear that I had the biggest penis in all of France!

Guy, the boss, took a shine to me. I was first in and last out, and I used to beg him to let me make the staff dinner. I wouldn't take my half-day off during the week. I would come in and work for nothing.

English customers would come, and Guy would say that they must be taken into the kitchen to meet me, his little British chef, because he knew how homesick, how isolated I was. He saw through my arrogance, my pushiness. I was like an orphan there, and he stepped in as a father-figure. People sometimes point out how, in shows like *Kitchen Nightmares,* I'll always encourage the youngest chap in the kitchen. If you want to know why – Paris is why. I know how it feels to be in a corner, unnoticed and unloved.

After I'd been in Guy's kitchen for a year, I told him I wanted to move on. That was when he offered me a job as his Number Two. I was thrilled, but, as a Number Two, I would have to show other people what to do, and I wasn't ready to finish my training so soon. So I went to the great Joël Robuchon, where – guess what? – I went straight back to being a humble commis.

Joël's restaurant, *Robuchon,* was the most famous restaurant in the world at the time. The kitchen was in a kind of corridor, and once you were installed there, you simply didn't move for the next five hours. Joël made Marco look like a pussycat. One evening, we had eight Japanese investors in: two wanted duck, two a meat course, and four fish. I'll never forget it. The duck was cooked wrapped in pastry. So that would come out of the oven, and then you had two minutes before the other main courses all had to be ready. Timing was crucial.

One of the fish I had to cook was hake. I had to wait until all the breadcrumbs were the same colour. Then I had to take it out and pipe on this butter. I was also doing John Dory and sea bass, all in two minutes, timing myself by a clock on the hearth.

All of a sudden, Bernard, one of the French chefs, had fucked up. There was a problem with the pastry, and he was in such a rage that he slammed the oven door and the glass broke. A minute later, I saw this huge copper pan coming at us, the pan that the duck was supposed to be in. It turned out that the meat section had panicked and forgotten to put the duck in it. Someone had lifted the lid up and discovered this, and, well, I've never heard a scream like it. The guy had to start again from scratch. It was horrific, and if there had been a back door, I think we all would have bolted.

Joël was such an unpleasant person to work for. On my last week, the fucker even put me on bin duty. You literally had to climb inside the bins on a Saturday morning and hose them down for about three hours. It was a terrible job.

'But it's my last day tomorrow,' I said to Chef.

'Look, you'll be here tomorrow morning, cleaning those bins out, or you'll never work in a Michelin-star restaurant again. I'll ring every chef in France and make sure that you're banned.'

That night, I knew I wouldn't get my money. I had worked the last month for nothing.

After my stint at *Robuchon*, I knew I was good for nothing. Not for a while, anyway, because, physically, I was broken, but I couldn't afford not to work. What I needed was a lucky break, a way of earning some cash and recharging my energy at the same time. That break came to me just in the nick of time. And this time, believe it or not, the money was good and the hours were human.

Chapter Five

Oceans Apart

A guy came into the restaurant who had an agency near Nice that employed chefs to work on board the yachts of millionaires. A few days later, I sent them my CV. Within twenty-four hours, they contacted me and told me that they had a job for me on board a charter. The idea of what amounted to a working holiday sounded like just what the doctor ordered. So I headed down to the Med. My boat was captained by an absolute knob, but berthed next to it was another boat, *Idlewood*. One night, I got talking to one of its deckhands, and he let me know that they were looking for a chef, too.

'Our captain's called Ginger Steve,' he said.

I met up with Ginger Steve two days later, and he told me that he worked for a high-profile couple, but that he couldn't tell me who they were, which meant that the owners had to be seriously rich. So, forty hours later, I'm sailing off into the sunset on this beautiful mega-yacht.

It was amazing. The kitchen was massive for a boat. There were twenty-two crew members, and I was earning about $4,000 per month, which is a fortune. And bear in mind that I was spending no money. I didn't even have to cook for the crew. My assistant did that.

It turned out that the boat was owned by Reg Grundy and his wife, Joy Chambers. Reg is one of Australia's most famous media bosses. He founded the Grundy Organisation, which makes television shows like *Young Doctors* and, most famously of all, *Neighbours*. Joy is a novelist and an actress. They were charming, the perfect employers, and I loved them to bits. I'm still in touch with them. They came to my restaurant *Aubergine* when it opened. They came to my wedding and they send my children presents.

After the summer season, I'd saved about £15,000, which seemed like a fortune, and I felt fantastic. But I was dying to get back to London and use everything I had learned to open my own restaurant. Then I was asked if I would travel with the boat across the Atlantic to the Caribbean. Then the Grundys would pay for me to fly back to Europe. When would I get the chance to do something like that ever again? I was torn between wanting to pursue my dream back in London or have one last adventure – so I agreed.

* * *

Cooking for the Grundys helped me to develop my style even further, strange as that may sound. They adored fine dining, but they were also health-conscious. So breakfast was stewed fruit, and dinner was light – no cream, no butter, even if there were important guests around the table. For me, it was great. I was being paid very well indeed to evolve my own culinary style. You can see traces of my time on the *Idlewood* in the way I cook now.

I had so much respect for Reg. We got on like a house on fire. He was so loyal to his staff, some of whom had worked for him for thirty-five years. He taught me the importance of looking after people long before I opened the doors of my own restaurant.

But I never let myself forget that this, for me, was just another leg in my journey. And I could feel myself getting closer to achieving my goal every day. I could almost SMELL that restaurant of mine. It was in my sights. I just had to reach out and grab it with both hands.

Chapter Six

A Room of My Own

I got a call from Pierre Koffmann, the chef and owner of a restaurant in Chelsea with three Michelin stars. His head chef had just walked out, and he wanted to know if I was interested in the job. Of course I said yes, even though what I was really after was a place of my own. At the time, that restaurant was the envy of every chef in London. That included my 'old friend' Marco, who was often on the phone pestering me to see him. One Friday night, I finally agreed.

Marco was going great guns at his restaurant, *Harvey's*, and he was involved in another restaurant called *The Canteen*, where he'd installed my old flatmate Stephen Terry as chef. Why did I agree to meet him? That's simple. He held out the biggest bait of all.

'How do you fancy your own restaurant?' he said.

I met him at *The Canteen*, and we jumped in a cab. He wouldn't tell me where we were going, but eventually we wound up in Park Walk. Then we walked into this restaurant. It was all galvanised steel and black paint.

Marco said, 'All this can be yours. My other partner at *The Canteen* – he owns it. It's losing ten grand a week.'

The following week, Marco told me that I could buy 25 per cent of the restaurant and reopen it as mine a week later. I was still only twenty-six, but I made my mind up quickly. I went to the Midland Bank and borrowed £10,000 for the restaurant, which I renamed *Aubergine*. Marco had no financial involvement in the deal. He was just setting it up. I knew he would have had his reasons but I was too excited to think about it much.

I started on a £22,000 salary, and I was meant to open the following week.

'Fucking hell,' I said to Marco. 'How am I supposed to open on the first of October when I've got no staff and no menu?'

'Don't worry,' he said. 'I'll help you.'

You'll be wondering why I wasn't more wary. I was just excited about having my own place. I didn't ever sit back and think: who's this? What are they up to? A lot of Italians got involved in the deal, but I never queried that. Just let me cook, I thought.

It was all very tough. But I had a good right-hand man – or at least I did in the end. The day before I left my old restaurant, Marcus Wareing came in. He and I had worked together before, and he was a great chef.

I didn't offer him a job there and then because I had no money to pay him, but as soon as I did, I brought him in.

So then there were three – me, Marcus and a junior chef. And later, of course, all the great chefs who are still with me now came through that kitchen. I didn't know it at the time, but *Aubergine* turned out to be the greatest training ground for chefs in Britain.

* * *

Meanwhile, my private life was getting tricky. I'd met Tana, who is now my wife and the mother of our four children, but she was going out with a friend of mine, Tim Powell. This was in 1993–4. Not long after we'd opened *Aubergine*, Tim and Tana came in for dinner. God, I thought, there's my mate with that stunning girlfriend of his, whom I'd met briefly a year before when he picked me up at an airport.

That evening, I cooked my heart out. Then Tana had a New Year's Eve party, to which I was invited. And there was Tim, telling me how his future father-in-law, Chris Hutcheson, Tana's dad, was going to set him up in a restaurant. Meanwhile, I'm in business with a bunch of Italians I'm not quite sure of.

About three months later, I heard that Chris had sent Tim off to New York for work experience with a famous American chef. I couldn't believe my ears: the little bastard was getting everything that I ever wanted. I buried myself in my work.

The only relief I could get was from my Yamaha motorbike. On a Saturday night, I'd meet all my mates, and we'd all pile out onto the M4. We'd sit on our petrol tanks and play dare to see who could hold their bike at full throttle, and keep it there from bridge to bridge. It was an amazing adrenalin rush, and the only way I could relax after work.

I couldn't afford to park this bike anywhere, but Tim and Tana had an amazing flat by the river, and Tim had said that I could park my bike in his garage there. It must have been early summer, June, when I went down there late at night to get my bike. I pressed the buzzer to the flat, and Tana answered. I'd left my keys at their place in case Tim had to move the bike during the week.

'Where's Tim?' I said.

'Didn't you know? Tim and I separated a week ago.'

'You're joking!' I said. I tried to seem sympathetic, but inside I was dancing a jig.

So, boom! I was straight upstairs. I didn't bother going to Soho to see my mates. Instead, I stayed with her, talking, until about six in the morning. Then I asked her if she fancied coming out on the bike with me. Tim had his own helmet somewhere. So, as dawn broke, we set off.

That was how we started seeing each other, and we married in December 1996.

Chapter Seven

War

We got our first Michelin star at *Aubergine* fourteen months after we opened our doors, in 1995. Two years later, in 1997, we got our second star. We went from nothing at all to two stars in just three years. Only one other restaurant in Britain had ever done that. Everyone came: Princess Margaret, David Bowie, Robert de Niro. We were so busy that not even Madonna could get a table.

It was around this time that my relationship with the Italians involved in the restaurant began to get difficult.

A few months after I got my first star, Marco told me that he needed to talk to me.

'My chef is leaving,' he said. 'I'm going to give you a share of the business, I'm going to make you my best of chefs, and I'm going to pay you £100,000 a year. You'll never need to worry about money again. Don't tell me now. I want you to think about it. Let's have dinner on Sunday night.'

Fuck me.

That Sunday, over dinner, I told him.

'That's an amazing offer,' I said. 'The thought of running your three-star restaurant is a huge honour. But I was with you at *Harvey's* when you got three Michelin stars, and, to be honest, all I want to do now is win three stars myself.'

His reaction was shocking.

'You're fucking mad,' he said. Then he started raving on about my Italian business partners, about how much debt they were in, and what their plans were for *Aubergine*.

'They're about to close it down,' he said. 'They're going to sell the restaurant, and you won't have a pot to piss in.'

So I went to my Italian contact. *Aubergine* was fully booked. We were taking forty grand a week, at least. Weren't we secure?

'We're not making any money, Gordon,' he said.

Then he gave his side of the story about Marco. Things had started to go wrong over at *The Canteen*, and not long after this, Marco quit.

Then some odd things started to happen. *Aubergine* picked up a bad review by Jonathan

Meades in *The Times*. At the time I thought that Marco might be somehow behind it, and I began to wonder if he was trying to get back at me for turning down his offer. I felt the same about a horrible review by A. A. Gill, the restaurant critic of *The Sunday Times*. A. A. Gill and Marco are best buddies, so it was easy to convince myself that they were working together. With hindsight, however, I now know this was just down to my paranoia. The stuff they were writing was so obviously rubbish, but still, I felt very nervous.

Then, out of the blue, the Italians told me that they wanted to open a second fine dining restaurant. As before, they would give me a 10 per cent share. All I had to do was find a chef. I immediately thought of Marcus Wareing, and we opened *L'Oranger* in St James's. It was a huge success, and won a Michelin star after just six months.

The next thing that happened was that other companies started sniffing round with a view to buying us. I wasn't interested in selling, but the Italians were. People started to tell me that Marco and the Italians were working together and that they were going to sell my restaurant without telling me. Marco, of course, denied this. With only a 10 per cent share, I would have had very little control.

To make things worse, Tana had just got pregnant with our first baby, I'd got myself a new mortgage, and I was up to my eyeballs in debt. I'd created this great restaurant, and I'd nearly killed myself doing it. I had worked at the stove for sixteen hours a day, and now it was about to be taken away from me.

The night that I came up with my master plan, I couldn't sleep. So I went up to a little café by Chelsea Bridge and got myself a cup of coffee and a bacon sandwich. Then I sat there all night, plotting how I could secure my bollocks. I needed an idea that would turn the Italians against Marco because, that way, all their plans would crumble to dust. And I needed to keep my own nose clean.

By morning, I had it. I would arrange for *Aubergine*'s reservations book to disappear, and to the Italians, at least, I would make it clear that Marco was to blame.

In the days before computers and the Internet, a top restaurant's reservations book was worth its weight in gold. We were fully booked between four and six months in advance, and the book had details of every single one of those bookings. Without it, the place would sink into total chaos. So that is what happened. I made it disappear.

Chaos followed. We had hundreds of calls from punters who didn't actually have reservations, but who were happy to try it on, knowing the mess we were in. The newspapers wanted details, and I was all too happy to do as many interviews as they wanted.

'Only someone in the trade would know the full value of a reservations book,' I told journalists.

Marco denied his involvement. Besides, who else would want our reservations book? Where did I keep the diary during all this? Oh, I had it in a very safe place.

The Italians were totally pissed off with Marco. They were right back on my side. I was relieved. I no longer liked Marco, and I no longer trusted or wanted him to 'help' me at the restaurant. It was my own place or nothing.

But I did string Marco along. He had taken over the restaurant at the *Café Royal*. He had this idea that he would go into partnership with Chris Hutcheson, by this time my father-in-law, and me, and let us run the *Café Royal*. We went along with it, but Marco didn't know that we had plans to buy another restaurant. Whenever Marco mentioned the *Café Royal*, I'd pretend to be interested, and whenever the Italians talked about my future with them, I'd smile and nod.

The smirk on my face must have been a mile wide. We had funding for the new restaurant, *Royal Hospital Road*. No one knew, but we were on our way to the real starting line.

Chapter Eight

The Great Walk-Out

The deal on *Royal Hospital Road* was completed – secretly, of course. I felt very excited. It was time for me to resign from *Aubergine*. This should have been easy, but, thanks to the Italians, it turned into one of the most dramatic moments in my career so far. One of the Italians, Giuliano, had bought out the others, and now had 90 per cent of *Aubergine*. But I still hadn't signed anything.

Giuliano wanted Marcus Wareing to sign a four-year deal with the company. So far, Marcus had refused. Then a small discrepancy was found in the food costs at *L'Oranger*. This gave Giuliano an excuse to turn on Marcus.

'Sign this fucking deal or I'm going to sack you,' he said.

Marcus didn't sign. So he was sacked and marched off the premises.

Then I gathered all of the staff around me, both from *L'Oranger* and *Aubergine*, and told them that I was going to stand by Marcus. I would resign as a director, and I was going to open a new restaurant.

'You're more than welcome to come and join me,' I said. 'I hope there'll be a job there for all of you, but at the moment, nothing is certain. If you want to hand in your notice and follow me, that's up to you. I can't tell you what's going to happen next, but, in my view, both these restaurants are finished.'

What happened next was amazing.

On the spot, forty-six members of staff walked out, and, in doing so, closed two of London's best restaurants.

Both *Aubergine* and *L'Oranger* were shut for several weeks while Giuliano tried to get new staff. That meant that the company was losing an awful lot of money. More than £100,000 a week was being spent in the two restaurants. Customers with reservations took their business elsewhere. Possible future customers did not want to eat in either place if their chefs were no longer in the kitchens.

Those restaurants *were* Marcus and me.

Of course, the press had a field day.

When I resigned, Giuliano was still saying that we could work things out, but I'd waited eighteen months to have my say, and I wasn't having any of it.

'Don't you know how hard I've been working over the last fucking year?' I said. 'My wife was pregnant with our first child, and we had all sorts of problems with that, and all that time you were trying to undermine me. I swear to God, I will never even think of doing business with you again. Now, you own these restaurants. Fuck off and run them!'

A few weeks later, on the first of September 1998, we opened the doors of my new restaurant, *Royal Hospital Road*. I found jobs for every single person who'd supported Marcus and me. It was thrilling. But our troubles weren't over yet.

* * *

Being issued with a writ is never what you'd call pleasant, but I was handed this one on my way back from my father's funeral.

Giuliano was going to sue me for a lot of money for breaching my contract by leaving *Aubergine* and *L'Oranger*. He also accused me of breaking my contract with him by stealing his staff. I was going to fight him all the way, even though I had no spare cash for legal fees.

Giuliano wanted revenge for what had happened after the Great Walk-Out. He was also furious because we planned to open a second restaurant just a few doors up from *L'Oranger*. We could afford to do that because things were going so well at *Royal Hospital Road*. In the January after we opened, *Aubergine* lost one of its Michelin stars and *Royal Hospital Road* gained two.

I had to sell our house to fight the legal battle, and we moved back to renting. That was a terrible thing to have to do. My childhood had made me long for a safe, secure home of my own. And I felt terrible for Tana, who had Megan, our new baby.

In the end, the judge strongly advised us to settle out of court. If we carried on, even the winner wouldn't get very much money. So, four months after I received the writ, we settled. I needed to work on my restaurants. We were on our way now, and we couldn't afford to let anything else stand in our way. And, as usual, I was broke.

Chapter Nine

The Sweet Smell of Success

In January 2001, *Royal Hospital Road* picked up its third Michelin star. On the same day, my wife handed me the keys to a blue Ferrari. Lovely as the car was, there is no doubt in my mind which one was the greater prize. I'd longed for that third star, and now all my hard work had paid off. It meant, officially, that my restaurant was the best in London because, the year before, two other chefs lost their three-star status. To this day, mine is still the only three-Michelin-starred restaurant in London.

My third star wasn't just important in its own right: it meant that bigger, better things were around the corner.

There were changes at Claridge's Hotel, and my father-in-law, Chris, went to a meeting. There he met a man who has amazing vision, John Ceriale. John immediately threw down a challenge by asking if I would be happy to do breakfast if we were to take over the restaurant at Claridge's, but there was a catch. I'd have to cook the breakfast.

Chefs hate doing breakfast, and Chris knew this, but it would be great to run the Claridge's restaurant, and other people would be interested in this. So Chris replied yes. Later, he told me that he had wondered how to break this news to me. He even said that, had it been a problem, he would have done the breakfasts himself. God forbid!

We were both thinking the same two things. First, that we were not going to lose out on this amazing opportunity, and second, a successful breakfast business would pay the rent, leaving the income from lunch and dinner to us.

A deal was struck. I would be allowed to put my name above the door, and, what's more, my restaurant would have its own entrance. I was thrilled. With its old-style glamour, Claridge's is a place I've always loved, and its history is amazing. It's been open in one form or another since 1812, and everyone has visited, from Queen Victoria to Margaret Thatcher, from Donatella Versace to David Beckham. The restaurant was very much a place I liked to take Tana, so I was determined to get everything completely right.

When it opened in October 2001, we had spent £2 million on furniture, decoration and all the rest. The room, in shades of my favourite aubergine, is airy and elegant. I chose all the china, glassware and cutlery myself.

I was determined to run our kitchen at *Claridge's* and the kitchen at *Royal Hospital Road* at the same time. I was lucky because I had a great right-hand man coming with me to *Claridge's*, Mark Sargeant. But the drive from Mayfair to Chelsea took just seven and a half minutes. If I had to, I could flit between the two.

We spent a lot of time practising our menus. We always trial new dishes over and over until they are perfect. As a result, the menu at *Claridge's* is exquisite.

Claridge's was an immediate hit. In our second week of trading alone, we welcomed some 1,500 guests. We were on our way, and I had proved something: it *was* possible to run more than one restaurant to the same high standard (the restaurant at Claridge's soon won a Michelin star).

My next project was to open a restaurant in Glasgow. That idea was very dear to me, for obvious reasons. I liked the idea of having a success there. So we opened a seventy-seater restaurant inside Glasgow's most popular hotel at the time.

Glasgow was the first British city to have a Versace store outside London. The city is very swish, so I felt there would be a market for our kind of cooking. I appointed David Dempsey as chef, and the food was brilliant. Within a year, this new restaurant had won a Michelin star.

In 2002, at the request of our business partners, we opened a restaurant in The Connaught hotel in Mayfair. The Connaught is a very special place – but its restaurant had become as stodgy as hell. I got Nina Campbell to redecorate it, and appointed Angela Hartnett as chef. She has an Italian background, and the menu was going to have a modern Italian touch – a real change for us. I agreed that our move into The Connaught could be filmed by the BBC2 behind-the-scenes series *Trouble at the Top*. This was good publicity, both for the restaurant and for Angela, who dealt with me and the cameras really well. The restaurant, once the complaints of some rich old ladies had died down, was a huge success. Angela's restaurant, which we called *Menu*, went on to win a Michelin star in 2004.

After setting up at The Connaught, which was not easy, I must admit that I did feel as if anything was possible. But, when the idea of us taking on *The Savoy Grill* came up, I couldn't quite believe it. The Savoy is probably London's most famous hotel. On a typical weekday, you could find any number of cabinet ministers dining at *The Savoy Grill*. It was very, very traditional. It still had a dessert trolley, for God's sake, heaving with trifles and jugs of buttercup yellow Jersey cream. Changing it was going to be like messing with the Holy Grail.

The American designer Barbara Barry gave the room a new sense of glamour – but it still felt like *The Savoy Grill*. In the kitchen was Marcus Wareing. Marcus combined a modern approach with the best features of the old *Grill* – the dessert trolley, for instance, and he continued to serve dishes like omelette Arnold Bennett. The critics loved it and so, too, did its customers.

Since *The Savoy Grill*, we have gone from strength to strength. The *Boxwood Café*, my take on an American diner, has been a huge hit, proving those who said that I can't do anything other than fine dining totally wrong. I was keen that it would have a child-friendly environment, and it is the only one of my restaurants where I'll allow my own kids to eat. The Knickerbocker Glories are worth crossing London for.

More recently, we opened *maze* in Grosvenor Square. Jason Atherton, its chef, won a Michelin star inside a year. I would say that the *maze* bar is one of the most glamorous in London.

Abroad, we opened two restaurants in hotels in Dubai and Tokyo.

It is now over a year since I opened in the hard, brutal world of New York. We opened in Florida around the same time, but that was simple, compared to the politics, union problems and food critics in New York. Now we are preparing for a big opening in Los Angeles. This, in many ways, will be as important and challenging as New York, and it will need all my time at first, and back-up from London.

Every time I open a new restaurant, the critics fill the newspapers with the same old stuff: I am spreading myself too thin, or this new restaurant has to do with vanity and money, rather than the passion that was behind *Aubergine*.

It's total rubbish. In the weeks building up to an opening, I am there, totally. I'm hands-on, putting the chefs through their paces, testing every dish, over and over. All my chefs have worked for me for years, and I trust them completely. People ask me who does the cooking when I'm not there, and my answer is always, 'The same people who do it when I am there.'

* * *

What makes me really pissed off in the kitchen? What makes me explode? Lies.

A chef can overcook a scallop, he can overcook a fillet of beef, but what he can't do is lie about it. It's not that he's lying to me. He's lying to the customers, too, and I won't have that.

The second thing I can't stand is dirty cooks. I want clean trousers, clean hair and clean nails. If a chef is proud about how he looks, he's proud about how he cooks. Since we brought in the idea of the Chef's Table – a table right in the heart of the kitchen, where customers can see all the action – this has been more important than ever.

We have a Chef's Table in all our fine dining restaurants now, and they're usually booked for months in advance. In 2002, Tony Blair celebrated his forty-ninth birthday at the Chef's Table in *Claridge's*. It's also been used by Andrew Lloyd Webber, Richard and Judy, Ronnie Wood and Kate Moss. That one table alone earns £1 million a year for our company.

The third thing I can't stand is clock-watchers. There's no room for clock-watchers in a kitchen. You could be working twenty hours on the trot. So what? That's the way it goes.

But there's one thing above all that I have grown to despise, and that is a fat chef. I should know. I was one myself once. That's why I started running. I did my first marathon in four hours and fifty-eight minutes. My best time so far is 3.30 and fifteen seconds, which I got in 2004. My dream is to break 3.30, and I can definitely do it.

How quickly can I tell if a new cook is going to be good enough? Within a day, is the honest answer, and inside a week you can see whether they're going to be with you for two years or five.

The easiest way for a new chef to impress me is with their seasoning. That gives me a real idea of what a cook's palate is like. You could be the most able cook when it comes to roasting a scallop or braising a turbot, but if you can't season what you're doing, you're lost.

What about women in kitchens? I love women chefs: they're intelligent, they're fast learners, and they can be tough. As for the effect they have on the boys, it's entirely good. Put a woman in a kitchen and discipline will improve. The guys hate being told off in front of the girls. It's a playground thing – they just find it embarrassing.

So how often am I in the kitchen myself? Well, in spite of the business and all the travel, my TV work, the recipes I write for *The Times* and my books, and all the other millions of drains on my time, I am still heavily drawn to my restaurants. Three to four nights a week I am at *Royal Hospital Road,* and for three to four lunches.

Royal Hospital Road is the top restaurant, but it only has twelve tables. That's forty seats. It's closed at weekends, and it's the same team for lunch and the same team for dinner. It's foolproof.

It's a perfect space – like eating inside a fucking Chanel handbag. It turns over £3 million a year, and makes between £500,000 and £750,000 a year in profit – all from this tiny little restaurant. To say that there's a waiting list for a table is less than half the story. Once the list is thirty to forty tables long, we have to stop taking names: it's just too embarrassing. They're never going to get in.

What makes a three-starred Michelin restaurant? Consistency. Every night must be to the same very high standard.

People tend to say, 'God, Christmas must be a nightmare for you.'

No, that's wrong. January is the same as December. May is the same as March. The menu is seasonal, and it changes between every ninth and twelfth week. We'll change half the dishes one week, the rest the next. Nothing must be left to chance because this is the jewel in our crown.

* * *

Of course, there have been failures. The Glasgow restaurant was brilliant, but Scotland is the home of the deep-fried Mars Bar and the deep-fried Nutella-fucking-sandwich.

The restaurant was always fully booked at weekends, but during the week this was not the case. It was a place Glaswegians went to only as a huge treat. As a result, in three years of trading, we lost £480,000. No chef, however brilliant, can keep a restaurant open on just two good nights a week. It affects quality as well as profit, because good cooks thrive on being busy – and so, in January 2004, the restaurant closed.

Since then, whenever we've been planning a restaurant in a new city, we've always been extra careful to do our research, to find out what people really want. In the future, I'd love to open another restaurant in Glasgow. I love the place, and I'm extremely proud of my Scottish roots. But next time, I think we'll go for something a little more informal. It's a case of horses for courses.

Chapter Ten

Welcome to the Small Screen

And so to the TV series *Hell's Kitchen,* one of the worst experiences of my life. The idea of the show was that I taught a group of celebrities to cook for real-life celebrity diners, with all the pressures of a busy restaurant. One of the celebrity chefs was voted off by the public every night.

I honestly had no idea of how big the show was going to be – the scale of the kitchen that they'd built or the size of the restaurant. ITV were offering me £40,000 an hour, so I would basically earn half a million pounds for two weeks' work.

As was obvious to anyone who saw even five minutes of the show, I wasn't too impressed when I met the contestants. To be honest, I didn't know who half of them were.

How was this lot going to cook food to a high enough standard to be served in a restaurant?

More to the point, how were they going to do it quickly enough?

I was furious with the production people for the amount they were allowing the contestants to drink late at night. This might have made some of the footage they got better, but I had a fucking restaurant to run. The battle lines were drawn. They were all supposed to be cooks, so I treated them like cooks.

The real problem was that the producers were only worried about making a 'reality' TV programme, and the contestants were only worried about how they looked on that programme, while I was attempting to run a proper fine dining restaurant. As for Angus Deayton, who was presenting the show, I soon found out that he was taking the piss out of me. They wanted me to chat to Angus on camera – you know, a bit of friendly stuff – but the show was live, so they couldn't make me. He was fucked then.

'Fuck off, Angus,' I could say. 'I'm not interested. I'm too busy.'

I went to ITV and I said, 'You're going to have to make big changes. You're going to have to get some proper chefs in to do some of the preparation.'

Then came my big bust-up with Amanda Barrie, the *Coronation Street* actress.

She physically tried to punch me. At that point, I walked.

I said to ITV, 'She's going to have to be removed. What are you waiting for? For someone to be stabbed?'

My walking out never came out in the press, but let me tell you now, all hell was let loose.

That night, I walked all the way home to Wandsworth, still in my chef's clothes. It was really weird. I felt completely spaced out.

I thought, 'If they're not going to listen to me, I'm not going to do this any more.'

The next day, on the Sunday, I just didn't show up, at which point ITV finally agreed to get some proper chefs in. And so I agreed to go back.

Jennifer Ellison, who won the show, worked well, no doubt about it. So did Al Murray. There was a level of respect there, and quite a lot of talent. To this day, he puts on amazing dinner parties. He's a fucking good cook. He takes it seriously.

The one who really got on my tits was Edwina Currie. There were members of the public (and even quite a few of my mates) voting to keep her in the show just because they loved watching her wind me up. She was just so fucking lazy and totally irritating.

The occasion for the big bust-up came when she didn't prepare her special.

It was about ten minutes past six when I said to Edwina, 'Where's your special? What are you doing today?'

'I haven't done it,' she said.

'Say that again.'

'It's not really my dish, and I don't like it, so I haven't done it.'

The production people were going mad.

I looked at her and I said, 'You're a fucking joke, aren't you?'

'I beg your pardon?'

'One minute you are shagging the Prime Minister, and now you are trying to shag me from behind.'

It just came out. I hadn't planned it at all. I knew how everyone was running around kissing her arse, totally scared of her. Well, I was not scared of Edwina Currie – a bully who shagged the Prime Minister. It was music to my ears when she finally got kicked out. The silly cow.

* * *

I was hugely relieved when the whole thing was over. Three days later, I was off to South Africa to run a double marathon. I pulled out after six hours. My legs were fucked. That was the first time I'd failed to finish a race, and it was all because of Edwina Currie. I was just exhausted. I had nothing left.

Soon afterwards, we had an email from Channel 4 saying that they wanted to do a second series of *Kitchen Nightmares*, the other TV series that I had been doing. The money they were going to pay me leapt from £50,000 to £100,000. I was amazed. Then ITV asked if I would do a second series of *Hell's Kitchen*. We heard that an American company was interested in the idea of doing the show, so I was off to Los Angeles to meet them. Two days after that, Channel 4 came in with a million-pound offer to keep me there. In the end, I did do the show in America, but I passed on the offer from ITV in the UK. Why? Lots of reasons. *Hell's Kitchen* didn't make much sense to me. I worried about the way it made people think about me, about the kind of attention it brought.

The show attracted lots of knobs, like the coughing major from *Who Wants To Be A Millionaire?* He started giving me shit. On ITV2, there was a programme of extra material from the show, which Jordan was presenting. Hilarious. There she was, walking up and down this red carpet, reading from a card held right up in front of her fucking nose.

'Hello, and welcome to *Extra Portions from Hell's Kitchen*.'

Laughable, really.

So why did I agree to do the same show in America? Simple. They wanted to do it without using so-called celebrities. The contestants were members of the public who seriously wanted to cook, and the prize for the winner, at least for the second series, was the chance to have their own restaurant in Las Vegas. In other words, it was a real, tough competition. I was in charge of the talent, and I could make all the decisions about cooking and food.

I've now signed for five seasons in America. I don't think there's a chef in the world who would have turned down the kind of money they've put into the show, and it has paid off. The ratings are amazing. It's a fantastic success. More importantly, it's given me a profile in the US that I could only dream of before.

Of course, after my television shows, I'm part of that strange celebrity world. So much of it is a pile of crap, though. We've had everyone in the restaurants, from Pierce Brosnan to Beckham, but we don't have special arrangements for celebrities. There's no secret telephone number for them.

Tana and I have become quite close to the Beckhams, and I do get frustrated when people are so wrong about them. When you get to know them, you realise how normal they are – and how normal they want to be. Compared to them, though, I've had an easy time from the press. The press have been nice to me. I try to work with them as much as I can. You have to look on it as a relationship, but it's a dangerous one.

Because of everything I've done, there are some amazing moments. I get lots of requests – will you come and cook at my house? One request was to cook for Blair and Russia's President Putin at Downing Street – which was a great thrill. There was a split second when I was standing between Blair and Putin – one of those moments when I couldn't help but think how far I'd come.

And there are my cookbooks. I see them very much as working with my TV shows. People see how to do the recipe on screen, and then, hopefully, they are interested and want to know more. So they go out and buy the book to try things at home.

I do use cookbooks myself. It's a myth that chefs don't. I own about 3,500. I pick them up everywhere I go. Can I learn anything new from all these books? Of course I can. You can use a book for ideas, but you can't learn to cook from books. That's impossible. There has to be some natural flair.

Whom would I recommend to the home cook? Nigel Slater, without a doubt. He's not a chef. He's a cook. He's never come into fashion and he'll never go out of fashion. He has a timeless quality, and he's good beyond belief.

But it's the restaurants that really do it for me.

Chapter Eleven

New York, New York

In early July 2006, I went to Holyrood Palace in Edinburgh to pick up my OBE from the Queen. I took Mum, Tana, and my daughter Megan – three generations of women from the same family. The award means a huge amount to me. It's just a little confirmation of how far I've come, that I'm doing okay. But the most important thing about it was that it was awarded to me for my services to the industry. It had nothing to do with my television work. I think that pleased me more than anything. I felt amazingly proud.

But it's certainly not the end. People often ask me whether there'll ever be a day when I've got enough restaurants in my group and enough Michelin stars under my belt. The answer to both questions is no. With regard to Michelin stars, another chef has got three three-starred restaurants, in New York, Monaco and Paris, so it's definitely possible. That's my goal.

Luckily, I've got some time up my sleeve, and my guys want it as well. Already, we have opened up successfully in Prague. Restaurants in the Trianon Palace in Versailles and in the Pulitzer Hotel in Amsterdam have only the final touches to be completed, and they will become part of our European growth, too.

Ah, yes. New York is the restaurant capital of the world. Our first restaurant in that fantastic city opened in November 2006, and making a success of it is the biggest, most important challenge of my career so far.

'We can't wait to see you go down in flames in New York,' read one anonymous email I received. 'We want the meat off your bones.'

The target in New York is three stars. The American *Michelin Guide* awarded us two stars last year, but I won't stop till it has earned three.

Do I think we can do it? Fuck me, yes, definitely.

* * *

People often ask me about the way eating habits have changed in the years since I became a chef.

I always say the same thing, 'Yes, they have, but there's a huge task ahead.'

I'm not convinced that people cook enough. We need to get back our feeling for ingredients, for running a kitchen budget. We need to get closer to what we eat, to look at it more, to love it and pay it attention.

So far, whatever anyone likes to think, the food revolution in this country has happened mainly in London. But that's not to say that I'm not hopeful that things will get better, slowly and surely. And I'm willing to play any part I can in making British habits change.

As you must know by now, I think good food is important. It can be life-changing.

Just look what it's done for me.

Quick Reads

Books in the Quick Reads series

www.quickreads.org.uk

Quick Reads

Pick up a book today

Quick Reads are bite-sized books by bestselling writers and well-known personalities for people who want a short, fast-paced read. They are designed to be read and enjoyed by avid readers and by people who never had or who have lost the reading habit.

Quick Reads are published alongside and in partnership with BBC RaW.

We would like to thank all our partners in the Quick Reads project for their help and support:

The Department for Innovation, Universities and Skills
NIACE
unionlearn
National Book Tokens
The Vital Link
The Reading Agency
National Literacy Trust
Welsh Books Council
Basic Skills Cymru, Welsh Assembly Government
Wales Accent Press
Lifelong Learning Scotland
DELNI
NALA

Quick Reads would also like to thank the Department for Innovation, Universities and Skills; Arts Council England and World Book Day for their sponsorship and NIACE for their outreach work.

Quick Reads is a World Book Day initiative.
www.quickreads.org.uk   www.worldbookday.com

Other resources

Free courses are available for anyone who wants to develop their skills. You can attend the courses in your local area. If you'd like to find out more, phone 0800 66 0800.

A list of books for new readers can be found on www.firstchoicebooks.org.uk or at your local library.

Publishers Barrington Stoke (www.barringtonstoke.co.uk), New Island (www.newisland.ie) and Sandstone Press (www.sandstonepress.com) also provide books for new readers.

The BBC runs a reading and writing campaign. See www.bbc.co.uk/raw.

RaW

2008 is a National Year of Reading. To find out more, search online, see www.dius.gov.uk or visit your local library.

www.quickreads.org.uk   www.worldbookday.com